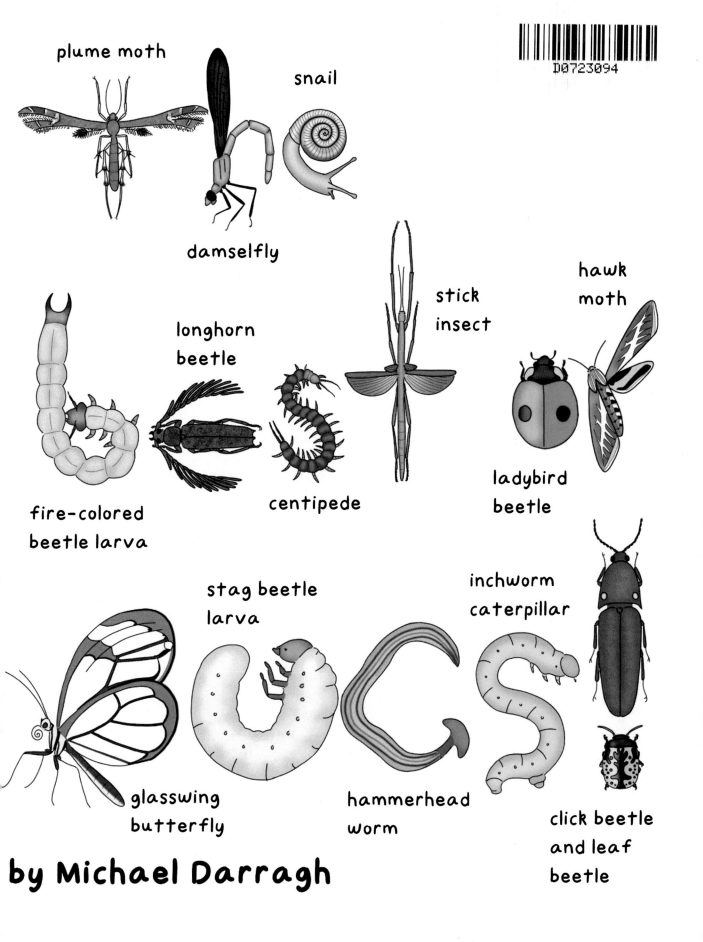

plume moth

snail

damselfly

longhorn beetle

stick insect

hawk moth

fire-colored beetle larva

centipede

ladybird beetle

stag beetle larva

inchworm caterpillar

glasswing butterfly

hammerhead worm

click beetle and leaf beetle

by Michael Darragh

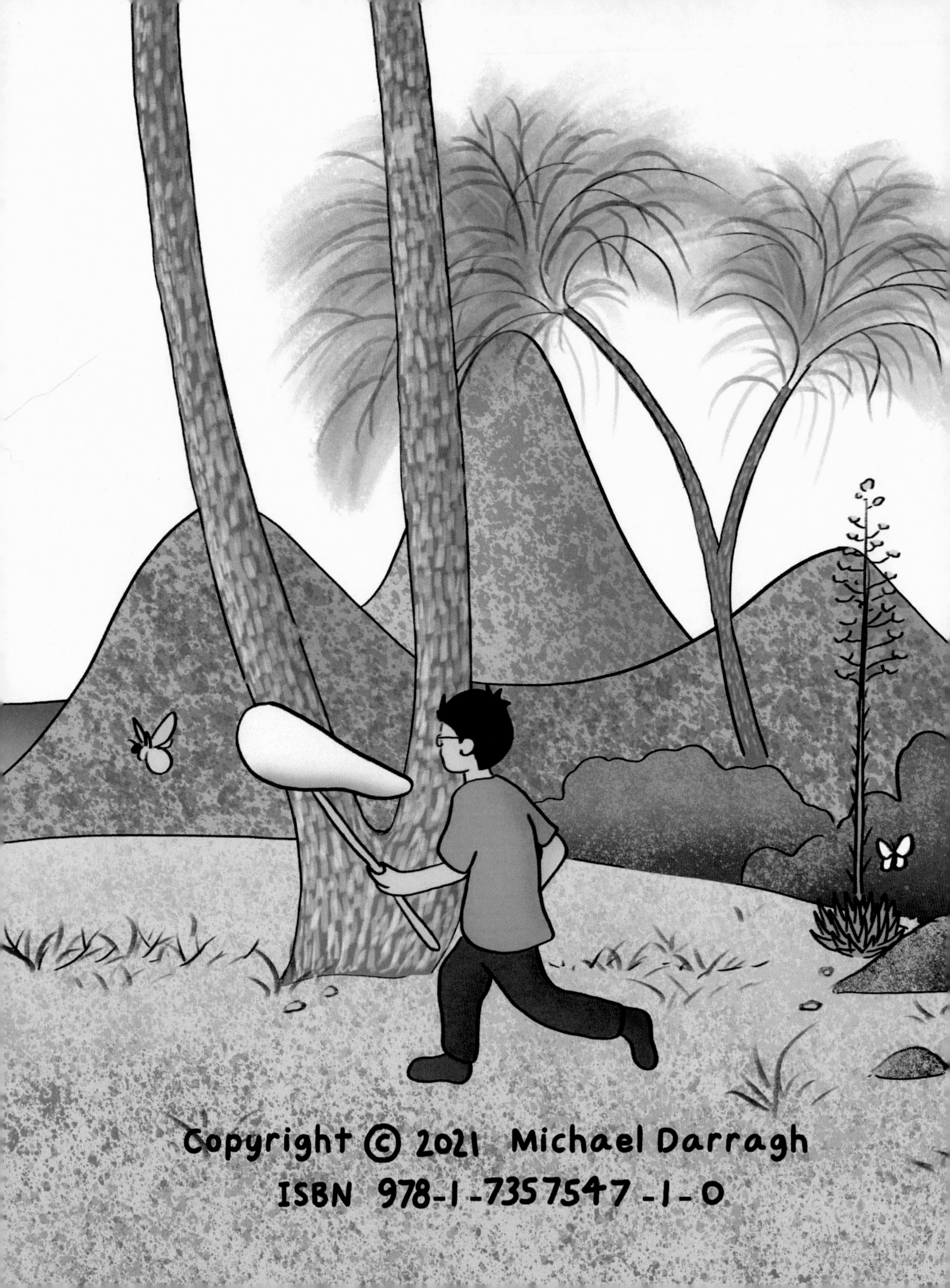

ISBN 978-1-7357547-1-0

For Renee, Russell, and Lauren

The world is full of insects. Each one begins life as a baby, just like you and me. Some baby insects look just like their parents, only smaller and without wings. They are called nymphs.

grasshoppers and crickets

dragonflies and damselflies

mayflies

praying mantises

stick insects

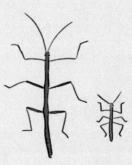

stoneflies

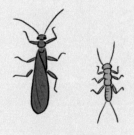

true bugs

earwigs

cockroaches

Other baby insects look very different than their parents. They are called larvae. Unlike nymphs, they have to spend time as a pupa before they become adults.

beetles

flies
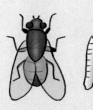

wasps, bees, and ants

moths and butterflies

fleas

dobsonflies and fishflies
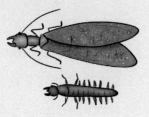

scorpionflies

net-winged insects

caddisflies

People are squishy on the outside and have hard bones on the inside. Insects are the opposite. They are hard on the outside and squishy on the inside. Their bodies are covered by a hard shell called an exoskeleton. To grow bigger, an insect larva needs to shed its exoskeleton and grow a new one that is larger. Here is the life cycle of a stag beetle:

First, a female stag beetle lays eggs near some good food for their babies. Baby stag beetles eat dead wood.

When the beetle larva comes out of the egg, it is very small. As it eats, it grows larger and larger. It sheds its exoskeleton two times before it is big enough to turn into an adult.

The third time the larva sheds its exoskeleton, it turns into a pupa. As a pupa, it does not eat. It just waits while its body changes from a larva to an adult. This process is called metamorphosis.

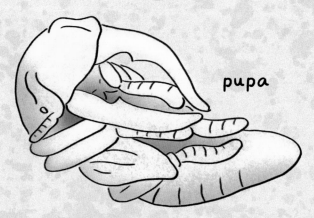

pupa

The adults of many insects eat different food than the larvae. Adult stag beetles don't eat wood like they did as babies. They eat tree sap instead. Some adult insects don't eat anything at all.

Stag beetle pupae are hidden away from danger inside wood. Other insect larvae, like moth caterpillars, build cocoons around themselves when they are ready to form a pupa. The cocoons help keep them safe!

adult male

How do you know an insect when you see one? It helps to count their legs. Insects have six of them. These animals have too many legs to be insects.

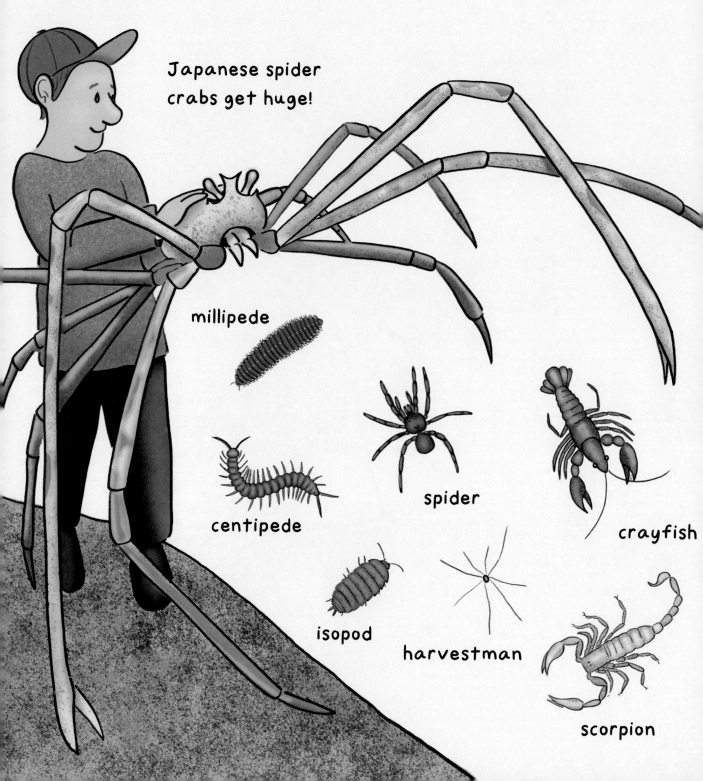

Japanese spider crabs get huge!

millipede

centipede

spider

isopod

harvestman

crayfish

scorpion

There are all kinds of different insects because insects do all kinds of different things. We can guess what an insect does from how it looks. Here is a picture of a mantidfly. It is not a praying mantis but it also catches insects using its front legs!

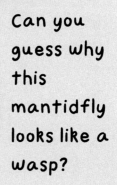

Can you guess why this mantidfly looks like a wasp?

mantidfly

mole cricket

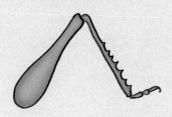

grasshopper

The legs of other insects are adapted for other things. The mole cricket uses its front legs for digging. The grasshopper hops with its hind legs. And the water boatman uses its long legs to swim.

water boatman

Most insects are small and shy but you can find them! Flowers are some of the best places to look. They provide nectar and pollen for pollinators like bees, butterflies, and beetles. Pollinators help plants by carrying pollen from one flower to another. Without them, plants would be unable to produce many of the fruits and vegetables we eat.

Insect predators know there are a lot of insects on flowers. You can find hungry spiders, praying mantises, and assassin bugs waiting there, hoping for a tasty treat to come along!

sweat bee with yellow pollen on its legs

tumbling flower beetle

crab spider

You can also find a lot of insects on the leaves and stems of plants. Some of the insects, like caterpillars, chew on the leaves.

Stick insects are good at disappearing among the branches.

hickory horned devil
Life size!

Wasps can be helpful by eating caterpillars that can hurt trees.

Other insects suck sap from leaves and stems. The poop of sap sucking insects is like sugary water and many insects come to drink it! If you find a plant with aphids, you will likely find ants visiting them to drink their sweet poop!

Why do you think this treehopper looks like a thorn?

Ants love aphid poop!

A lot of insects are beneath our feet. Many of them are in dead leaves and the top layer of soil. If you dig a hole you can find them. The deeper you dig, the fewer insects you will find.

hawk moth pupa

Cicada nymphs live underground where they feed on roots. Some stay down there for seventeen years before they become adult cicadas!

Yellow jackets build their papery nests in holes underground. Don't get too close!

Moles are experts at finding insects, worms, and other tasty treats in their dark underground tunnels.

Many insects build their nests underground. They can dig little rooms where they will be safer from predators. If you look closely, you can find the holes leading to their underground tunnels.

queen
ant
laying
eggs

scarab beetle larvae eating grass roots

Bee larvae eat balls of pollen their mom collects from flowers. Once they have eaten all the pollen, they will be ready to become adult bees!

Woodpeckers know a dead tree is a good place to find insects! But they have to work hard to find them.

This wasp uses a long tube to lay eggs inside beetle larvae hidden in the wood.

flat bark beetle

stag beetle

pseudoscorpion

hove fly

termites

flat bug

click beetle larva

Many insects in dead trees are small and flat so they can squeeze under bark. Others are huge! The biggest beetles in the world live in dead wood!

This eyed click beetle has a pseudoscorpion riding on its back. That is how they get around!

The titan beetle from South America is the biggest beetle in the world. The larvae feed on dead wood.

Life size!

Mushrooms growing on dead wood attract a lot of brightly colored fungus beetles.

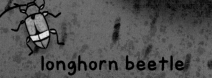

longhorn beetle

Thousands of different kinds of dung beetles eat poop. Many of them bury balls of poop underground for their babies to eat. Some roll balls of poop away so no one steals them! Without these beetles, the world would be a messy place! Farmers like dung beetles because if they didn't remove the poop, there wouldn't be as much grass for cows and other animals to eat.

This beetle will bury this ball of poop after rolling it away.

This beetle buries balls of poop directly underneath the main pile of poop.

This is one of the largest kinds of dung beetles. It feeds on elephant poop. I wonder what kinds of beetles ate dinosaur poop?

Life size!

Once an animal dies, insects come and lay their eggs on it. It is good food for their babies. Flies are some of the first to come. Many beetles come too. If you ever find a dead animal, you can watch how quickly it gets eaten by insects. When burying beetles find a small dead animal like a mouse, they bury it. That way nothing can steal it from their babies!

Fly larvae are called maggots. They look like little white worms and grow very quickly.

burying beetles

Did you know some insects and spiders can walk on water? Others are good at swimming. Many insects are like turtles and must come to the surface of the water to breathe. Others are like fish and can breathe under water using their gills. Many insects stay in water only while they are young. When they become adults, they have wings and can fly above the water.

Water striders live on the water surface. They eat other insects including mosquito larvae.

Whirligig beetles swim in circles on the water surface. They can see what is going on under water and in the sky at the same time!

Diving beetles carry bubbles of air under their wings for breathing.

Like fish and baby salamanders, damselfly nymphs use gills to breathe under water.

gills

dobsonfly larva

gills

baby salamande

When dobsonflies grow up, they leave the water and fly away. Males have giant jaws!

Life size!

damselfly

fishing spider

giant water bug

mayfly nymph

Caddisfly larvae build little homes to live in!

Some insects are only found in tree holes.

Flower chafer larvae feed on rotten wood in dry tree holes.

Hide beetles live in owl nests.

Click beetle larvae eat other insects.

Scirtid beetle larvae eat dead leaves in wet tree holes.

Dry hole with an owl nest

Wet hole, full of water

breathing tube

Some hover flies are only found in tree holes. Their larvae breathe through long tubes that stick out of the water!

Sucking water out of a tree hole is a good way to find mosquito larvae. Many of them eat little particles of food in the water. You can feed them fish flakes from a pet store.

Mosquito larvae hang upside down in the water and breathe through small tubes. Mosquito pupae breathe through tubes on their backs.

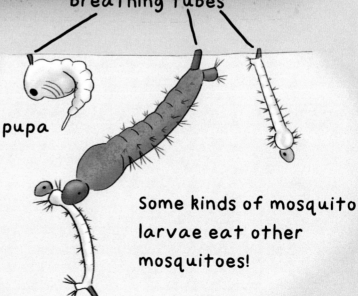

breathing tubes

pupa

Some kinds of mosquito larvae eat other mosquitoes!

One place you won't find insects is in the ocean.
Millions of years ago, when insects came along,
the ocean was already full of
animals. There may have been less
danger and more food
on land than in the sea at that
time. If the first insects
had gone into the ocean,
they would have seen
something like this:

crinoids

early fish

bryozoa

cephalo

horn coral

clams

Sea scorpion

spon

brachiopods

trilobites

Insects can often be found in the nests of birds and other animals. They are also found in our homes and even on us!

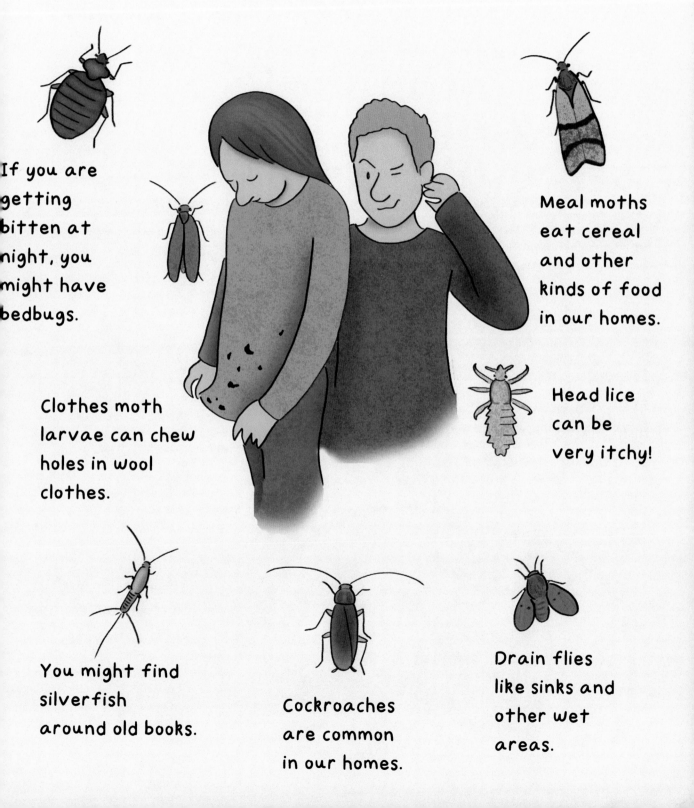

If you are getting bitten at night, you might have bedbugs.

Clothes moth larvae can chew holes in wool clothes.

You might find silverfish around old books.

Cockroaches are common in our homes.

Meal moths eat cereal and other kinds of food in our homes.

Head lice can be very itchy!

Drain flies like sinks and other wet areas.

Some insects can sting or bite. Wasps, bees, and other insects use their stingers to protect themselves. Some also use their stingers to hunt for food. They don't want to sting us but will if they think we might hurt them.

Tarantula hawk wasps use their stingers to hunt. They feed tarantulas to their babies.

Some caterpillars have stinging spines. The spines help protect them from birds and other predators.

This beetle from South America has stingers on its antennae. They look and work just like a scorpion's stinger!

Most insects are too small or shy to hurt us. Some of them are very gentle. Mother earwigs take very good care of their babies. They clean the eggs and feed the nymphs after they hatch!

If you look carefully under rocks, you may find an earwig mom watching her babies!

Looking for insects is always a fun way to spend the day. Do you have a net? If not, you can make one with a pillow case, a clothes hanger and a stick! If you bring a jar, you will have something to put insects into so you can get a good look at them. Here are a few more ideas that might help you.

Many insects only come out at night. You can use a flashlight to find some of them. The best way to see them is to shine a bright light on a white sheet. They will come to the light.

You can also make traps for insects. You can make a pitfall trap by burying a cup in the soil. Insects that fall in can't get out! You can hang different kinds of smelly food above the cup and see what comes.

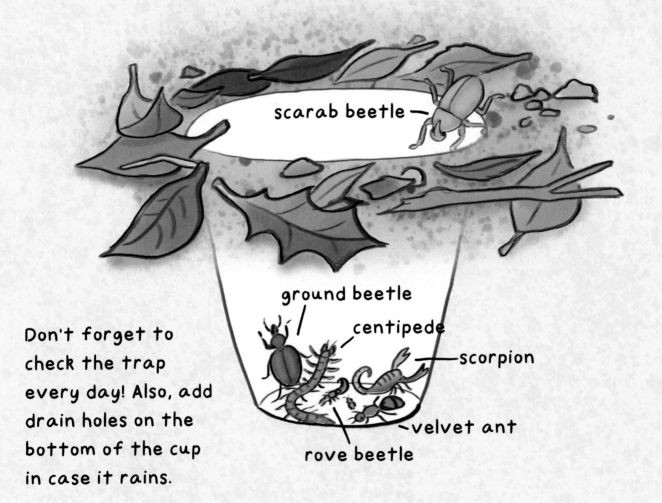

scarab beetle

ground beetle

centipede

scorpion

rove beetle

velvet ant

Don't forget to check the trap every day! Also, add drain holes on the bottom of the cup in case it rains.

You can also make a window trap. Insects that fly into it will fall into the bucket below. Try putting the traps in different places to catch different kinds of insects! To make one, attach a clear plastic window to a plastic bucket. If you add a funnel to the bucket, insects can't get out. Don't forget to check the trap every day!

clear
plastic
window

Funnel so the insects don't fly out

bucket

Made in the USA
Coppell, TX
15 May 2021